Animal Dens

THERESE HOPKINS

PowerKiDS press
New York

Published in 2009 by The Rosen Publishing Group, Inc.
29 East 21st Street, New York, NY 10010

Copyright © 2009 by The Rosen Publishing Group, Inc.

All rights reserved. No part of this book may be reproduced in any form without permission in writing from the publisher, except by a reviewer.

First Edition

Editor: Nicole Pristash
Book Design: Kate Laczynski
Photo Researcher: Jessica Gerweck

Photo Credits: Cover, p. 1 © James Hager/Getty Images; p. 5 © www.istockphoto.com/John Pitcher; pp. 7, 9, 11, 21, 23, 24 Shutterstock.com; p. 13 © Thorsten Milse/Getty Images; p. 15 © Stephen J. Krasemann/Getty Images; p. 17 © www.istockphoto.com/Yan Gluzberg; p. 19 © Panoramic Images/Getty Images.

Library of Congress Cataloging-in-Publication Data

Hopkins, Therese.
 Animal dens / Therese Hopkins. — 1st ed.
  p. cm. — (Home sweet home)
 Includes index.
 ISBN 978-1-4358-2698-4 (library binding) — ISBN 978-1-4358-3072-1 (pbk.)
ISBN 978-1-4358-3084-4 (6-pack)
 1. Animals—Habitations—Juvenile literature. I. Title.
 QL756.H787 2009
 591.56′4—dc22
                    2008025233

Manufactured in the United States of America

CONTENTS

Animal Dens 4

Fox Dens 6

Caves 10

Rocky Dens 14

Words to Know 24

Index 24

Web Sites 24

A den is a place where foxes, bears, **cougars**, and wolves live. These wolves are sitting in front of their den.

A den can be a hole on the side of a hill, like this fox den.

Foxes raise their babies in their dens.

A **cave** is another place that can be used as a den.

Polar bears live in icy caves in the snow.

A den can also be a space in between rocks.

15

Brown bears live in the **mountains** and between large **boulders** in the forest.

Animals use their dens to keep their young safe. This cougar is resting with her babies in her den.

Wolves use their dens to watch out for other animals.

A den is also a good place to sleep. This wolf is taking a nap in its den.

WORDS TO KNOW

boulders

cave

cougar

mountains

INDEX

B
bears, 4, 16

C
cave, 10, 12
cougar, 4

M
mountains, 16

W
wolves, 4, 20, 22

WEB SITES

Due to the changing nature of Internet links, PowerKids Press has developed an online list of Web sites related to the subject of this book. This site is updated regularly. Please use this link to access the list:
www.powerkidslinks.com/hsh/dens/